YOUR KNOWLEDGE H

Bibliographic information published by the German National Library:

The German National Library lists this publication in the National Bibliography; detailed bibliographic data are available on the Internet at http://dnb.dnb.de .

Imprint:

Copyright © 2017 GRIN Verlag, Open Publishing GmbH
Print and binding: Books on Demand GmbH, Norderstedt Germany
ISBN: 9783668567740

This book at GRIN:

http://www.grin.com/en/e-book/379630/taxpayers-rights-in-comparative-perspective-the-protection-of-tax-related

Nadja Büngers

Taxpayers Rights in Comparative Perspective. The Protection of Tax Related Information of Individual Taxpayers and the Rationale Behind It. A comparison between the legal systems of Germany and the United States

GRIN Publishing

GRIN - Your knowledge has value

Since its foundation in 1998, GRIN has specialized in publishing academic texts by students, college teachers and other academics as e-book and printed book. The website www.grin.com is an ideal platform for presenting term papers, final papers, scientific essays, dissertations and specialist books.

Visit us on the internet:

http://www.grin.com/

http://www.facebook.com/grincom

http://www.twitter.com/grin_com

Submission Date: 14 July, 2017
Name: Nadja Büngers
Word Count: 8442

Taxpayers Rights in Comparative Perspective:
The Protection of Tax Related Information of Individual Taxpayers and the
Rationale Behind It.

A comparison between the legal systems of Germany and the United States

Thesis
To obtain the academic degree
Bachelor of Laws

Abstract

Taxpayers are obliged to file their annual returns which the state needs to fund its expenses for society. By doing so, sensitive and personal information are disclosed to the respective tax administration. Inevitably, the issue of disclosing relevant information arises as well as the question of how to treat the information without harming the basic rights of an individual taxpayer. This thesis contributes to the issue of disclosing tax related information by focusing on tax confidentiality, its development and status, the current legal framework, and the rationale behind the approaches of tax confidentiality, undertaken by different legal systems. More specific, this thesis incorporates a comparison between the jurisdictions of Germany and the United States, examining their national legislative rules on tax confidentiality. By elaborating upon the similarities, differences, and the rationale of tax confidentiality in both systems, the thesis will uncover the fact, that both, Germany and the U.S. have a high level of confidentiality. There exist, however, interesting differences related to the level of confidentiality, and this thesis will conclude that the German system has a higher level of confidentiality, for instance in relation to the exceptions to tax confidentiality.

Keywords: Tax confidentiality; tax compliance; tax transparency; rationale; taxpayer privacy.

Abbreviations

AO -	Abgabenordnung, (Fiscal Code of Germany)
F3d. –	Federal Reporter, Third Series
F2d. -	Federal Reporter, Second Series
IRC-	Internal Revenue Code
IRS -	Internal Revenue Service
FOIA-	Freedom of Information Act
StGB –	Strafgesetzbuch (German Criminal Code)
StStatG -	Gesetz über Steuerstatistiken (Law on tax statistics)

Table of Contents

Introduction 5

I Germany 7

    Historical Development of Tax Confidentiality 7

    Legal Framework of Tax Confidentiality 9

        § 30 (1) and § 30 (3) AO – The Scope of Tax Confidentiality 10

        § 30 (2) AO – Breach of Duty 11

        § 30 (4) AO – Exceptions to Tax Confidentiality 11

        § 30 (5) AO – Disclosure in case of Intentional False Statements 13

        § 40 AO – Actions contrary to the Law 13

        Consequences of a Violation of § 30 14

II United States of America 14

    Historical development of Tax confidentiality 14

    Legal Framework of Tax Confidentiality 18

        Freedom of Information Act and Internal Revenue Code 18

        § 6103 (a) and § 6103 (b) IRC - Definitions 19

        § 6103 (c) IRC – Disclosure of Returns and Return information to designee

        of Taxpayer 20

        § 6103 (h) (4) IRC – Disclosure in juridical and administrative proceedings

        20

        § 6103 (m) – Disclosure of Taxpayer Identity Information 22

        § 6110 IRS – Public Inspection of Written Documents 22

III Comparison 22

    Historical Development of Tax Confidentiality 23

    Confidentiality as a right – Status in Constitution 24

    Legal Framework of Tax Confidentiality 24

    Possible Exceptions to Tax Confidentiality 25

    Violation of Tax Confidentiality 26

IV Rationale 27

Conclusion 29

Bibliography 32

Introduction

The collection and access of required tax information, as operated by the tax administration, must be ensued without compromising basic taxpayers' rights.[1] Especially, since financial and sensitive information of an individual are involved, the protection of information should have a strong manifestation in every legal jurisdiction.[2] This thesis contributes to the issue of how states cope with the problem of disclosing tax related information, by focusing on tax confidentiality.

The terms 'tax information', 'tax transparency' and 'tax confidentiality' are crucial concepts, which are used throughout this thesis. For the sake of clarification, hereinafter, their notions will be examined.

Tax information in general contains the income of a taxpayer. Besides this, however, tax information, encloses other details about personal circumstances, for instance expenses, personal belongings, savings, disability, and health status.[3] Inevitably, the publication of tax information does not only lead to a disclosure of income, but also of personal details of the individual taxpayer. This can comprise the taxpayer's private sphere.[4] The scope of tax information varies, depending on the legal system.

Both, tax transparency and tax confidentiality, relate to the right of the public to access the information that is held by tax authorities.[5] More specific, the former implies the right to access information that is found in a public administration.[6] A government, operating under a high level of transparency keeps all its information available for the public and offers insights into the process of tax assessment. In contrast, a government, which is considered to act confidentially, has a lower level of transparency.[7] Tax confidentiality, on the contrary, means that tax authorities do not disclose information to the public and

---

[1] Kristoffersson *et al.* 2013 (p.1), p. 1.

[2] United Nations Conference on Trade and Development 2016, p. iii.

[3] Würtz 1999 (p.1), p. 8.; I.R.C. § 6103 (b) (2).

[4] Blank 2012, p. 267.

[5] Hambre 2015, p. 166.

[6] Ernst & Young 2013, p. 7.

[7] Russell 2015, p. 1.

in principle regard the information to be secret.[8] In other words, it refers to the restricted access of sensitive information by the public.[9] It is important to note, that tax confidentiality is not considered to be a generally protected human right.[10] Nevertheless, it is an important value and most countries follow the approach of requiring tax authorities to keep taxpayers' information secret.[11] Moreover, the majority of states penalize tax officials that reveal confidential information.[12] It is essential to clarify, by what means different jurisdictions handle the issues that could result in a possible violation of the private sphere of taxpayers. This thesis aims at providing an insight on the approaches established in the legal systems of Germany and the United States (hereinafter U.S.). Its intention is to capture a full picture of the means taken by these jurisdictions, including their background and their rationale for their particular approach. There are significant discrepancies from a national law comparative perspective, which are not detectable at a first glance. The comparison revolves around the following question:

How are tax related information of an individual taxpayer protected by confidentiality, and what is the rationale behind it?

By answering this question, similarities and differences between the jurisdiction of Germany and the U.S. will be clarified and a basis will be created for comparative conclusions. This thesis goes beyond a descriptive approach, in that it will analyse the systems, and clarify the rationales behind the current approaches taken by both, the German and U.S. jurisdiction. The legal systems of Germany and U.S. were selected for the comparison due to the assumption that both have a high level of tax confidentiality. The intention is to explore the differences that cannot be recognised at first and to find out the reasons behind these approaches.

Part I will start with the examination of tax confidentiality under the German legal system. It will elaborate upon the historical development of confidentiality, followed by an explanation of the current tax law provisions in the

---

[8] Kristoffersson *et al.* 2013 (p.1), p. 3.

[9] Kristoffersson *et al.* 2013 (p.1), p. 3.

[10] Kristoffersson *et al.* 2013 (p.1), p. 5.

[11] Kristoffersson *et al.* 2013 (p.1), p. 5.

[12] V. Thuronyi 2016, p. 207.

Fiscal Code of Germany. The approach taken by the U.S. regarding tax related information, will be examined in Part II, starting with a brief presentation of the historical evolution of tax confidentiality. Afterwards, the focus will be placed on the relevant provisions of the Freedom of Information Act[13] and the Internal Revenue Code.[14] Subsequently, Part III will compare the approaches enacted by Germany and the U.S. and Part IV will explain the rationale of tax confidentiality in both countries. Finally, a conclusion will be drawn related to similarities and differences between the German and U.S. approach of tax confidentiality, which will provide an illustration of an overall opinion about the issue and the answer to the research question.

I Germany

Historical Development of Tax Confidentiality

Under German law, the term tax confidentiality, namely *'Steuergeheimnis'*, was established in 1933.[15] Its fundamental aspects, *per se*, were codified already 160 years ago. Dating back to 1851, the Prussian Income Tax Code was established, implying the provision on tax confidentiality in Section 32 of the Act.[16] Moreover, tax confidentiality was already protected by criminal law, which entails that a violation of confidentiality would result in juridical, criminal proceedings.[17] In the years preceding World War I, the legislative instruments that were enacted, followed the approach on tax confidentiality taken by the Prussian Law.[18] Tax confidentiality was implemented, inter alia, in the Income Tax Act of 1906 and in the *'Reichsgabenabordnung'* of 1919, which remained applicable for 60 years. [19] In this Act, tax confidentiality was stipulated in § 10. The court established in the *'Popitz Erlass'* of 09.11.1923, how tax confidentiality was

---

[13] U.S.C. § 552.

[14] I.R.C. § 6103 & § 6110.

[15] Koch & Wolter 1958 (p.1), p. 3.

[16] Valta *et al*. 2013 (p. 443), p. 444.

[17] Würtz 1999, (p.1), p. 3.

[18] Koch & Wolter 1958 (p.1), p. 3.

[19] Ax *et al*. 2007 (p.1), p. 6.

applied.[20] Under the regime of the national socialists, from 1933 till 1945, the importance of the protection of tax confidentiality was emphasized.[21] Notwithstanding, the practical approach of tax confidentiality did not appear to be the same as the theoretical approach. Lists of taxpayers, who filed their return late, were published. Besides that, tax confidentiality was often abused within situations in which the state acted according to its own interests.[22] After 1945 and with the end of World War II, one of the goals of the new government was to re-create tax confidentiality and to ensure that the abuse of tax confidentiality would not occur again.[23] The legislator codified exceptions that officially stated the circumstances allowing for a disclosure.[24] As a result of this arrangement, the legislator expressed that in order to disclose information and in order to justify a breach of tax confidentiality, a legal decree was required.[25] The enactment, thereafter, namely the codification of the Fiscal Code of Germany of 1977, contained tax confidentiality in § 30.[26] Even though, several amendments have been made since 1977, the Code remains, until today, the applicable law in relation to tax confidentiality.[27]

One can depict that the development of tax confidentiality in Germany has been characterized by a continuous improvement of the concept itself.[28] The following part will clarify the specific legislation, *lex specialis*, illustrating a more detailed approach of tax confidentiality in tax related laws of Germany.

---

[20] Metzger & Weingarten 1989, (p.168), p. 169.

[21] Koch & Wolter 1958 (p.1), p. 6.

[22] Koch & Wolter 1958 (p.1), p. 5.

[23] Koch & Wolter 1958 (p.1), p. 5.

[24] Koch & Wolter 1958 (p.1), p. 6.

[25] Koch & Wolter 1958 (p.1), p. 6.

[25] Koch & Wolter 1958 (p.1), p. 9.

[26] Ax *et al.* 2007 (p.100), p. 100.

[27] Pfaff 1974 (p.1), p. 3.

[28] Pfaff 1974 (p.1), p. 3.

Development of Tax Confidentiality

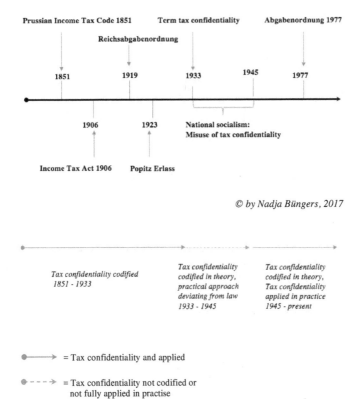

© *by Nadja Büngers, 2017*

● ──── → = Tax confidentiality and applied

● ‑ ‑ ‑ → = Tax confidentiality not codified or
              not fully applied in practise

© *by Nadja Büngers, 2017*

Legal Framework of Tax Confidentiality

The rules governing tax confidentiality in the German legal system are manifested in the Fiscal Code, called *Abgabenordnung* (hereinafter AO), which was enacted by the German *'Bundestag'* and published in 1977.[29] Since then, several smaller amendments were made to some of its provisions. The focus of this analysis will be placed on the last version of the AO, as published in 2017.

---

[29] Ax *et al.* 2007 (p.1), p. 6.

The AO contains rules for tax procedures, ranging from tax assessment, collection, and the enforcement of taxes to remedies and penalties in the case of tax infringements.[30] The provisions, relevant for the thesis topic are §§ 90, 93, 97, 30, and 40 AO.

Taxpayers are obliged to support the tax authorities in the tax assessment procedure by sending full statements of their tax affairs and personal circumstances to the administration. This obligation is stated in § 90 AO. Considering the cooperation with tax authorities for the collection of information, tax cooperation can be regarded as the counterpart of tax confidentiality.[31] Other forms of cooperation are found in § 93 AO, which explains the consultation of the taxpayer, in case of a significant departure from the facts stated in the tax return to the detriment of the taxpayer.[32] Moreover, § 97 prescribes that taxpayers are obliged, upon request by the tax authority, to provide relevant documents to the tax authority for the tax assessment.[33] Chapter four of the Fiscal Code offers the provisions on tax confidentiality. More specific, § 30, is of important relevance for the issue at stake as it provides the conditions for tax confidentiality.

§ 30 (1) and § 30 (3) AO – The Scope of Tax Confidentiality

§30 (1) AO stipulates the obligation of public officials to observe tax confidentiality.[34] Derived from this section, it can be discerned that the scope of the obligation covers public officials. Taking a look at § 30 (3) (1), the notion of public officials is examined by referring to the definition of Criminal Code, §11 (1) (4) StGb.[35] In addition to this section, the definition of public officials can also be found in §7 of the AO, which entails that a person, under the special obligation to civil services, is considered a public official.[36] Furthermore, §30 (3) refers to persons with an equivalent status to public officials, namely officially consulted

---

[30] Federal Ministry of Justice 2016, p. 6.

[31] Koch & Wolter 1958 (p.1), p. 6.

[32] Petersen 2005, p. 104.

[33] § 97 AO.

[34] § 30 (1) AO.

[35] § 30 (3) AO and §11 (1) (4) StGb.

[36] § 7 AO.

experts[37] and holders of church offices as well as other religious communities being public law entities.[38]

§ 30 (2) AO – Breach of Duty

§30 (2) elaborates on the breach of the duty to observe tax confidentiality and in which moment it constitutes a violation.[39] This section states that the obligation of tax confidentiality is breached if circumstances of a third person, *'Verhältnisse eines Dritten'*, are disclosed without authorisation. Those information have been received during official responsibilities, namely in administrative procedures, criminal proceedings or through the notification of another authority.[40] The meaning of 'circumstances of a third person' is neither defined in the provision, nor in a different provision of the Fiscal Act. The term 'circumstances of third persons' does not cover tax related data solely but also the tax base of any particular person and information about general financial and personal circumstances. [41] Furthermore, these circumstances include all personal, financial, economic, and tax information that have become known to the tax authority.[42] Another violation of the obligation of confidentiality is established when a corporate or commercial secret is disclosed without authorisation[43] or in the case of data, protected under the tax confidentiality section, being electronically retrieved unofficially.[44]

§ 30 (4) AO – Exceptions to Tax Confidentiality

§30 (4) entails four possible exceptions to the general rule of tax confidentiality that justify a disclosure of tax related information. [45] In order to reach justification, however, the provision must explicitly state a permission for

---

[37] § 30 (3) (2) AO.
[38] § 30 (3) (3) AO.
[39] § 30 (2) AO.
[40] § 30 (2) (1) AO.
[41] Ruegenberg 2001 (p.1), p. 28.
[42] Pfaff 1974 (p.1), p. 26.
[43] §30 (2) (2) AO.
[44] §30 (2) (3) AO.
[45] Würtz 1999 (p.1), p. 10.

the disclosure of the information.[46] In case the information serves the implementation of the information in administrative, criminal or tax proceedings, the first exception to tax confidentiality applies.[47] . The second exception to the rule of tax confidentiality applies, if a law exists that permits the disclosure of tax information. For instance, tax information is allowed to be disclosed for tax statistic purposes, as stated in the law for tax statistics of 1966.[48] Another exception to confidentiality exists when the taxpayer has given his consent that the information can be published.[49] This means that a taxpayer has the opportunity to waive his right of confidentiality.[50] There is no protection for a taxpayer, who does not want to own such a protection, as decided by the Financial Court.[51] Consent can be given orally, written, personally or through a representative person.[52] The fourth exception allows disclosure of information if it is serves the implementation of criminal proceedings for a crime, that is not a tax crime.[53] However, disclosure is only permitted, if the information have not been offered by the taxpayer, as obligation of his cooperation duty for the tax assessment.[54] Moreover, only information that was retrieved in criminal proceedings or administrative tax procedures is allowed to be used.[55] Furthermore, in case the taxpayer waived his right to withhold information, a disclosure is allowed.[56] The provision refers to situations, in which the taxpayer has been informed about his rights and the current investigations.[57]

§30 (4) (5) prescribes that in case there is a compelling public interest, like wilful crimes and serious offences against life and limb, the disclosure of

---

[46] Ax et al. 2007 (p.100), p. 104.

[47] §30 (4) (1) AO.

[48] § 9 (1) StStaG.

[49] § 30 (4) (3) AO.

[50] Pfaff 1974 (p.1), p. 47.

[51] BFH, 25.04.1967, VII 151/60, § 3.

[52] Würtz 1999 (p.1), p. 11.

[53] § 30 (4) (4) AO.

[54] Ax et al. 2007 (p.100), p. 107.

[55] § 30 (4) (4) (a) AO.

[56] § 30 (4) (4) (b) AO.

[57] Ax et al. 2007 (p.100), p. 107.

information may be allowed.[58] A list of serious offences can be found in §138 of the Criminal Code. This provision lists the examples of offences against life and limb or the state, for instance the preparation of a war of aggression, counterfeiting money or securities, economic crimes and murder under specific aggravating circumstances.[59]

§ 30 (5) AO – Disclosure in case of Intentional False Statements

§ 30 (5) illustrates that intentional, false statements of an individual may be disclosed to the law enforcement authorities.[60] In other words, if the taxpayer declares untruthful statements, the protection of confidentiality is automatically lost.[61] Moreover, the disclosure will not redact the identity of the taxpayer, implying that the name will be published as well.[62] This rule was established for law enforcement authorities to investigate manipulations, which otherwise would fall under the tax confidentiality provision.[63]

§ 40 AO – Actions Contrary to the Law

Another interesting provision is § 40 AO, which states that it shall be immaterial for taxation when a taxable action violates a statutory regulation or is contrary to public policy.[64] Hereby, the law emphasizes that even though the taxable object comes from an illegal source the taxpayer is supposed to disclose this information and the state keeps it confidential. In other words, the focus of this provision lies on the taxation of taxable objects, no matter what source they stem from. In case of an illegal source, for instance money gained from drug dealing, it is taxable and should be disclosed to the tax authorities, in order for the state to assess a complete taxation.

---

[58] § 30 (4) (5) (a) AO.

[59] § 138 StGb.

[60] § 30 (5) AO

[61] Ax et al. 2007 (p.100), p. 108.

[62] BFH, 08.02.1994, VII R 88/92, § 22 & § 23.

[63] Würtz 1999. p.14; § 355 StGb.

[64] § 40 AO.

Consequences of a Violation of § 30

If § 30 AO is violated by a public official or someone with an equivalent status, § 355 of the Criminal Code is applicable. This provision states that the person should be liable to imprisonment of two years or an equivalent fine. [65]

To sum it up, German law, on one side, is rather lenient in allowing data collection and entails the duty for the taxpayer to cooperate with the tax authorities. On the other side, it sticks to a rather strict tax confidentiality obligation in its tax administration. [66]

II United States of America

Historical development of Tax Confidentiality

Under the law of the United States, the evolution of tax confidentiality already started 150 years ago dating back to the outbreak of the Civil War in 1861. [67] Due to the financial crisis and a lack of state funds during the war, the Congress introduced the Income Tax Act in 1861. [68] In the following year, provisions were added to the aforementioned Act, which allowed for the public access of taxpayers' names and their liabilities. [69] Hence, during that time, it was not unusual that tax information was despatched at walls of courthouses and that newspapers published tax information of various persons. [70] In 1870, the Congress prohibited the public disclosure and codified this prohibition in the Revenue Act. [71] The Revenue Act contained a provision, which referred to the prohibition of disclosure of income returns and return related information. [72] Nonetheless, it also named the exception to this rule, namely in case of general statistics, which were regulated by the Commissioner of Internal Revenue. [73]

---

[65] § 355 StGb.

[66] § 40 AO.

[67] Blank 2012, p. 265.

[68] Pollack 2014, p. 297.

[69] Hambre 2015, p. 199.

[70] Department of the Treasury 2012, p. 1-1.

[71] Blank et al. 2013, p. 1167.

[72] Department of the Treasury 2000, p. 16.

[73] Hambre 2015, p. 199.

The Revenue Act of 1870 remained the applicable law until the enactment of the Tariff Act in 1909.[74] This Act contained a provision that permitted corporate returns to be made public but it was amended in 1910 due to uncertainty and conflicts with other provisions.[75] This amendment introduced the disclosure of information, which was solely allowed upon the order of the President of the U.S. and in conformity with the regulations that were endorsed by the Secretary of the Treasury.[76] The legal framework of confidentiality changed again, when the Revenue Act was introduced by the Congress in 1913. This Act enclosed a provision, which stated that corporate returns were public but individual returns enjoyed absolute tax confidentiality.[77] In 1924, the Congress codified a regulation offering a limited disclosure for individual tax returns. According to its provisions, the name of the taxpayer, address, the amount of tax paid, and tax funds were permitted to be published.[78] Moreover, by looking at case law, it can be recognised that the U.S. Supreme Court confirmed the right of newspapers to make lists of taxpayers' public.[79] In *US v Dicky*, the following is stated: *'(...) to authorize the Commissioner of Internal Revenue to make available for public inspection lists showing names of taxpayers and amounts of taxes paid by them'*.[80]

The Regulation of 1924 was amended in 1926 by declaring that only name and address remained open for disclosure, not the amount of tax paid anymore.[81] Due to the stock market crash in 1929 and the following financial crisis, the Congress began to think about means, which would prevent tax evasion and the abuse of potential loopholes.[82] This resulted in another enactment of the Congress, implying a limited measure of disclosure, the so called 'Pink Slip Requirement'.[83] It entailed that taxpayers were obliged to add a pink sheet of paper to their tax

---

[74] Twight 1995, p. 365.

[75] Department of the Treasury 2012, p. 1-2.

[76] Blank *et al.*, p. 1167.

[77] Department of the Treasury 201, p. 1-4.

[78] Hambre 2015, p. 200.

[79] Hambre 2015, p. 200.

[80] *United States v Dickey* 268 US 378 (1925) 386.

[81] Department of the Treasury 2012, p. 1-6.

[82] Blank *et al.* p. 1168.

[83] Act of 1934, Statute 680 & 698.

returns, which contained data as net income, gross income, tax liability, and deductions.[84] The pink slip was supposed to be available to the public.[85] However, due to extensive debates about its appropriateness and various safety concerns, the Act never entered full effect and was repealed in 1936. [86]

Until 1976, tax returns were therefore considered as public records, solely, if regulations applied and it was approved by the President or under presidential order. [87] Under these circumstances, many agencies had the opportunity to gain access to tax information, held by the IRS. [88] These rules were not reconsidered for 40 years, only after the impeachment proceedings against President Nixon during the 1970s.[89] The Nixon government used the IRS to access tax return information and used them for illegal ends.[90] The debate arose whether the abuse of privacy by the Nixon government would hinder the effectiveness of the voluntary assessment system of the U.S. As a response, the Congress enacted the Tax Reform Act in 1976, which contained a general provision against the disclosure of information that is collected by the IRS.[91] Afterwards, tax returns as well as return information have been treated as confidential and have been subject to disclosure exceptionally when authorised by statute.[92] The intention of the Congress, while creating this Reform Act, was to allow disclosure only when it is authorized by statute.[93] Moreover, the Congress attempted to balance the agencies need for the information with the citizen's right for privacy. [94]

Overall, it can be pointed out that the U.S. treatment of tax information ranges from a wide accessibility of documents, in the beginning of tax

---

[84] Blank *et al*. p. 1168.

[85] Lenter & Shackelford & Slemrod 2003, p. 809.

[86] Lenter 2003, p. 809.

[87] Berggren 1999, p. 825.

[88] Hambre 2015, p. 201.

[89] Hambre 2015, p. 201.

[90] Blank 2012, p. 278.

[91] Blank 2012, p. 279.

[92] Schwartz 2008, p. 893.

[93] Hambre 2015, p. 207.

[94] Department of the Treasury 2012, p. 1-9.

confidentiality, to a restricted approach on public disclosure, which is still applicable today.

Development of Tax Confidentiality

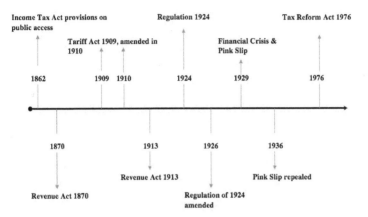

© by Nadja Büngers, 2017

Provision on public access to tax relevant information 1861-1870	Disclosure of tax relevant information prohibited 1870-1909	Provision on disclosure allowed upon the order of the President and in conformity with regulations of the Secretary of Treasury 1910 - 1913	Individual tax information treated confidentially 1913 - 1924	Limited disclosure for individual tax returns In 1926 – only name and address was allowed to be disclosed 1924 - 1976	Provision on tax confidentiality 1976- present

→ = Tax confidentiality and applied

--→ = Tax confidentiality not codified or not fully applied in practise

© by Nadja Büngers, 2017

Legal Framework of Tax Confidentiality

Freedom of Information Act and Internal Revenue Code

The Tax Reform Act of 1976, as mentioned above, was enacted as a response from the preceding events of the Nixon Government, after an immense debate arose about the misuse of accessible tax information.[95] Besides this, another reason for its enactment was the intention of the Congress to cope with the tension of the requirement for tax information and the citizen's right to privacy.[96] Moreover, the influence of disclosure on the continuation of tax compliance within the voluntary assessment system was addressed by the Congress during the creation of this Act.[97] The provisions of this Act are still applied today.[98] In the following paragraph, the current content on tax confidentiality will be illustrated in detail.

The applicable U.S. law, with respect to tax confidentiality, is the Internal Revenue Code (hereinafter IRC) and the Freedom of Information Act (hereinafter FOIA). Those legal instruments are interrelated and govern the approach of tax confidentiality.[99] The FOIA was enacted in 1966 to clarify and protect the right to information as a right held by the American citizens.[100] The FOIA prescribes the right of any person, to gain access to federal agency records and it is considered as enforceable in court. According to the Court in *Renegotiation Board v Bannercraft Clothing*, the purpose of the Act was rather the disclosure of information than confidentiality.[101] Nonetheless, in this case, the Congress recognised the importance of citizens' interest, especially the right to privacy.[102] Analyzing the provisions of the FOIA, the general obligation, manifested in § 552, stipulates that every federal authority that is requested for records, should make the records available for the requesting person.[103] This rule applies, unless one of

---

[95] Department of the Treasury 2012, p. 1-8.

[96] Department of the Treasury 2012, p. 1-9.

[97] Hambre 2015, p. 201.

[98] Blank 2012, p. 279.

[99] Department of the Treasury 2000, p. 4.

[100] Senate Report No. 813 (1965), p. 36.

[101] *Renegotiation Board v Bannercraft Clothing* 415 US 1 (1974) 17.

[102] Senate Report No. 813, 89th Congress, 1st Session (1965), p. 36.

[103] 5 U.S.C. §552.

the exemptions, stated in §552 (b), is valid.[104] The Court ruled in *FBI v Abramson* that the exemptions, named in the FOIA, must be 'narrowly construed', meaning that the list in § 552 cannot be expanded.[105] Article §552 (b) subsection (3) entails two required conditions for the exemption to be applicable. Namely, the exemption, as a first condition, holds that information is not disclosed, in case there exists another statute, which necessitates the information to be withheld from public, meaning that there is no discretion whatsoever.[106] The second condition requires that the other statute, which requires the information to be withheld from public, prescribes principles or measures, which are used for the withholding.[107] These two conditions are fulfilled by §6103 of the IRC, which is the entry point of Federal tax law. American Courts agree in their decisions upon the fact that §6103 is covered by the exemption of the FOIA. This can be underlined by looking at the Court's argumentation in *Renegotiation Board v Bannercraft*[108] and *Church Scientology v IRS*.[109] Moreover, the Internal Revenue Manual states that exemption §552 (b) (3) is mandatory and the IRS does not have any discretion in this respect.[110]

Provision §6103 refers to the Confidentiality and Disclosure of Returns and Return information. Since both conditions of §552 (b) (3) are satisfied, tax information is, by statute, exempted from disclosure and the rules laid down in the FOIA.

§ 6103 (a) and § 6103 (b) IRC - Definitions

The general rule holds that the return and return information of a taxpayer sent to the IRS, are treated confidentially. § 6103 (a) IRC names three categories of persons, who are prohibited to disclose return information; namely, officers and employees of the state, officer and employees of any state and persons, who, in

---

[104] 5 U.S.C. §552 (b).

[105] *FBI v Abramson* 456 US 615 (1982) 630.

[106] 5 U.S.C. §552 (3) (A).

[107] 5 U.S.C. §552 (3) (B).

[108] *Landmark Legal Foundation v IRS* 267 F3d. 1132 (2001) 1134.

[109] *Church Scientology v IRS* 792 F2d. 146 (1987) 150.

[110] Internal Revenue Service 2017, Part 11, Chapter 3, Section 13 (7) (4).

general, have access to return information. Those three groups are obliged to keep information confidential.

The definition of a tax return is anchored in § 6103 (b) (1), whereas the definition of return information can be found in § 6103 (b) (2). On the one hand, notion of return includes any tax return, which is required to be filed by the taxpayer.[111] Return information, on the other hand, covers almost all information that was referred to the IRS by the taxpayer regarding the taxpayer's liability under the Code.[112] Although, tax returns and their related information must be kept confidential, exceptional circumstances exist, which allow for disclosure of information, manifested in §6103 (c) to (o). In the following, three exceptions will be examined, which are of utmost interest on the topic of this thesis, namely: §6103 (c); §6103 (h) (4) and §6103 (m).

§ 6103 (c) IRC – Disclosure of Returns and Return Information to designee of Taxpayer

Starting with §6103 (c) the rule of tax confidentiality does not apply, if the taxpayer gives consent to the disclosure of his information. The consent must be written and signed by the taxpayer.[113]

§ 6103 (h) (4) IRC – Disclosure in Juridical and Administrative Proceedings

Another exception is stated in §6103 (h), which prescribes that a disclosure is permitted for the tax administration during the process of the tax assessment.[114] According to §6103 (h) (4), a return or return information may be disclosed in a judicial or administrative proceeding in relation to tax administration.[115] It stipulates that disclosure is permitted in judicial or administrative proceedings, if the taxpayer is a party to the proceedings or if the proceedings arose from the liability of the taxpayer. Referring to this provision, the question arises whether return information remains protected by the IRC, in case it was disclosed in

---

[111] I.R.C. § 6103 (b) (1).

[112] *Church Scientology v IRS* 792 F2d. 153 (1987) 158.

[113] Office of the Treasury Inspector General for tax administration 2015, p. 4.

[114] I.R.C. § 1603 (h).

[115] I.R.C. § 1603 (h) (4).

judicial and administrative processes.[116] This issue was addressed by a number of courts which came to different opinions.

On the one hand, the Court decided that information which was published, would still be protected by the IRC, for instance in the case of *Rodgers v Hyatt*.[117] Furthermore, in *Johnson v Sawyer*, the Court concluded that tax return information that is published results in a violation of §6103 (h) 4, no matter if it was a public record before. [118] The Court literally stated that 'Section 6103's protection does not disappear simply because tax return information has become disclosed in the public record.' [119] Again in *Mallas v US*, the Court concluded that the information remains confidential, independently of the source that made it public.[120]

On the other hand, however, in *Rice v US*, the court ruled that disclosure of information in press releases was not prohibited since it was not the IRS that published the information.[121] Moreover, in *Rowley v US* the Court came to the conclusion that once tax information is already in the public domain, the confidentiality protection of §6103 is automatically lost.[122] In those cases, the focus of the Courts was placed on the literal meaning of §6103 since it does not include public records as an exception and therefore, public records constitute a violation.[123] The majority of cases appear to conclude that disclosure of information of public records is allowed, since this information is not held by the IRS.

As a matter of fact, the situation in relation to this article is not clear- cut. The IRS argued in favour of this argument stating that tax information, which is found in the public record, does no longer enjoy confidentiality in connection with tax administration.[124]

---

[116] Hambre 2015, p. 213.

[117] *Rodgers v Hyatt* 697 F2d. 899 (1863) 906.

[118] *Johnson v Sawyer* 120 F3d. 1307 (1991) 1321.

[119] *Johnson v Sawyer* 120 F3d. 1307 (1991) 1321.

[120] *Mallas v US* 993 F2d. 1111 (1994) 1120.

[121] *Rice v US* 166 F3d. 1088 (1999) 1091.

[122] *Rowley v US* 76 F3d. 796 (1996) 801.

[123] Hambre 2015, p. 214

[124] Internal Revenue Service 2015, Part 11, Chapter 3, Section 11 (13) (3).

§6103 (m) – Disclosure of Taxpayer Identity Information

§6103 (m) implies another exception.[125] This provision prescribes that the IRS is permitted to publish tax information, which identifies the taxpayer to the press if the taxpayer, who is alleged of tax infringements, cannot be located. In this case, the IRS is permitted to send the information to the media. However, this provision does not entail that the IRS is generally permitted to disclose return information, which identifies individuals that are convicted of tax infringements.[126]

§ 6110 IRS – Public Inspection of Written Documents

Another interesting provision is § 6110 on Public Inspection of Written Documents. It states that tax information, related to written determinations and judgments, are available for public inspection.[127] Moreover, it covers information like rulings, guidance, chief counsel advise and other forms of written determinations. [128] The provision was added to the Internal Revenue Code through the Tax Reform Act of 1976; [129] it is assumed that the publication of these rulings inevitably increases public confidence in the tax system in that it acts fairly and treats everybody equal.[130] In order to publish, the identity of taxpayer, the name, must be redacted.[131]

Overall, it can be observed that the tax confidentiality approach taken by the U.S. implies a high level of tax confidentiality, however, in some aspects, the provisions are not clear-cut and questions remain.

III Comparison

The following Part consists of a discussion about the similarities and differences between the two legal regimes' tax confidentiality legislation. It offers considerations in relation to the legal systems at large. The comparison is drawn

---

[125] I.R.C. § 6103 (m).
[126] I.R.C. § 6103 (m).
[127] I.R.C. § 6110.
[128] Mehany & Michel & Rizek 2015, p. 883.
[129] Department of the Treasury 2000, p. 4.
[130] Hambre 2015, p. 210.
[131] I.R.C. §6110 (c) (1).

by looking at the aspects of evolution, constitutional aspects and the specific provisions on tax confidentiality.

Historical Development of Tax Confidentiality

In Germany, the right to confidentiality was introduced in the Prussian Tax code in 1851 for the first time and its provision remained rather static since its first appearance. Thus, it can be stated that the nowadays existing provisions are rooted in the Code of 1851.[132] Throughout the 21st century, the provision of tax confidentiality was codified as prohibiting disclosure. Although, tax confidentiality was codified during the regime of the national socialists, its provision was abused and sometimes ruled out, in the interest of the state.

As examined in this thesis, the development of tax confidentiality by the United States fluctuates. Between 1862, when the first tax confidentiality provisions were introduced by the Congress and 1976 when the Tax Reform Act was enacted, the level of confidentiality was modified several times. The whole development of tax confidentiality has been accompanied by the debate on whether to disclose taxpayer's information or not, by taking into consideration on how to arrive at tax compliance.

Comparing the historical development of tax confidentiality in Germany and the United States, it can be observed that the provision of tax confidentiality in the United States was inconstant, whereas in Germany tax confidentiality was permanently codified. The debate on the introduction of tax transparency, as opposed to, keeping tax confidentiality arose in the United States several times, due to the issue of tax compliance. On the contrary, this debate did not occur in Germany.

Even though, the provision of tax confidentiality in Germany between 1933 and 1945 was not properly enforced in practice. It can be concluded that the development of tax confidentiality in Germany is more static compared to the United States, which changed from disclosure to the protection of confidentiality.[133]

---

[132] Ax *et al*. 2007 (p.1), p. 6.

[133] Ax *et al*. 2007 (p.1), p. 6.

Confidentiality as a right – Status in Constitution

Another aspect, when comparing the two legal systems, is the legal status of tax confidentiality, taking into consideration the Constitution. Before analyzing the Constitution, however, it is essential to state that both legal jurisdictions, Germany and the United States, recognise tax confidentiality as a right, held by the citizens. This is proven by the provisions, which are anchored in the Fiscal Code of Germany[134] and the Internal Revenue Code[135] in the United States.

In both jurisdictions, the provision of tax confidentiality, however, cannot be found in the constitutional regime. In Germany, the Federal Constitutional Court decided that the right to confidentiality, is not regarded as having constitutional status, since it is no constitutional right.[136] Under U.S. law, the right on tax confidentiality cannot be found in the constitution and thus, has no constitutional status.

In fact, both, Germany and the United States, codified their provision on tax confidentiality in statutory law. Whereas under German law, the right to confidentiality is manifested in § 30 of the Fiscal Code, in the United States the right is codified in the Internal Revenue Code, namely in § 6103.

Legal Framework of Tax Confidentiality

In Germany, as stated above, the relevant tax confidentiality provision can be found in the Fiscal Code, more particularly, in §30. The general rule is the right of confidentiality, restricting public access. The obligation of confidentiality applies to public officials and persons having an equivalent status. § 30 AO refers to the disclosure of 'circumstances of a third person'. However, the notion of these terms is neither defined in the article, nor in a different provision of the Fiscal Code of Germany. The possible exceptions are stated in § 30 (4) AO, entailing four exceptions. However, next to the tax confidentiality, the Fiscal Code emphasises in §90 the duty of the taxpayer to cooperate with the tax authorities.

As elaborated earlier, when taking a look at the issue of tax confidentiality in the U.S., the analysis consists of the Freedom of Information Act and the

---

[134] § 30 AO.

[135] I.R.C. § 6103

[136] BVerfG, 17.07.1984, 2 BvE 15/83, § 5b.

Internal Revenue Code. Thus, § 6103 of the IRC is considered an exemption to the FOIA, since the conditions of §552 (b) are satisfied. Following that, provisions §6103 and §6110 are the relevant paragraphs for tax confidentiality. § 6103 prescribes the right to confidentiality of tax returns, return information, and the actual definitions of the term 'tax return' and 'return information' are included in § 6103 (b) (1) and § 6103 (b) (2). Furthermore, § 6103 contains the possible exceptions to the right of confidentiality, listed in § 6103 (c)-(o) that authorize disclosure in particular circumstances. Moreover, § 6110 makes the text of any written determination, which is issued by the IRS, available to public inspection, however, only redacted.

Thus, one conclusion is that even though the provisions of both presented tax confidentiality systems appear to be similar in their structure, the provision which is entailed IRC is clearer with respect to the actual scope and definitions of the article, in that it explains, what kind of information of the taxpayer is meant by the provision itself. Moreover, whereas under German law the cooperation obligation of the taxpayer is highlighted in §90, in U.S. law, the whole tax assessment is based on the voluntary compliance of the taxpayer and not on the cooperation duty of the taxpayer.[137]

Possible Exceptions to Tax Confidentiality

Germany, has the exceptions of the following cases: If the tax information serves the implementation of administrative or criminal proceedings, another statute permits the disclosure, consent is given by the taxpayer, the information is used for non-tax proceedings or in case of public interest. Moreover, when intentional false statements are investigated, the tax authority is allowed to disclose the information as well.

As mentioned in the foregoing Part, there is a total number of thirteen possible exceptions to the right of confidentiality in the United States. Disclosure is permitted if the consent by the taxpayer is given and if the taxpayer, who committed tax evasion cannot be found by the IRS, the information is transmitted to the media. Moreover, the disclosure of tax information is allowed in case it serves the implementation in judicial or administrative proceedings with respect

---

[137] Flora v United States 362 U.S. 145 (1962) 176.

to tax administration. In relation to §6103 (4) (h), the question remains whether information, which was disclosed in administrative or judicial proceedings, still falls under the protection of the IRC. This section offers a aberration from the high level of confidentiality, since the way it is interpreted influences the decision of whether the disclosure of information constitutes a violation of tax confidentiality or not. The opinion in this regard is split, in that some cases of the Courts support the argument, that is, indeed, is still protected. Therefore, the legal situation of the protection of returns and return information in this regard is not clear- cut.

This leads to the conclusion, that the situation of exceptions in the U.S. is rather unclear, compared to the German provision. This is due to the fact that the German provision exactly states, when information is protected, and when not. It is not dependent on the decisions of the Court, as it is in the U.S. Another aspect is that the tax administration in Germany is under no exception allowed to disclose taxpayer's information to the media, whereas in the U.S. it is allowed in case the taxpayer cannot be located.

Violation of Tax Confidentiality

On the one hand, in case of an unlawful disclosure of the 'circumstances of a third person', under German law the person is sentenced, according to § 138 Criminal Code, with two years imprisonment or a fine.[138] On the other hand, in the United States, §7213 is applicable, which perceives the violation of tax confidentiality as a felony, and states a fine up to 5000 dollars and up to five years imprisonment.[139]

This difference can be explained by the different approaches regarding the obligations of a taxpayer. In Germany, the taxpayer is, according to §90, obliged to cooperate with the tax authority, whereas in the U.S. the system is based on voluntary compliance. Therefore, in order to reach the voluntary compliance, taxpayers face a risk of being penalized to a higher degree in the U.S.

---

[138] § 138 StGB.
[139] I.R.C. § 7213.

IV Rationale

The following part will explain the rationale, which stands behind the approaches taken by the legal systems of Germany and the United States.

Under the legal regime of Germany, as examined above, the obligation of cooperation for the taxpayer exists. This implies that the taxpayer is responsible to disclose all his tax relevant information to the tax administration. The taxpayer is obliged to work together with the tax authorities during the tax assessment procedure, as reflected in the provisions of the Fiscal Code.[140] This cooperation is seen as the counterpart to the confidentiality requirements, which are the responsibility of the state.[141] In return, the state returns this 'trust' to the taxpayer, in that it keeps information confidential.

When evaluating the rationale of the approach that Germany adopts regarding tax confidentiality, the protection of the individual taxpayer is most important. This can be underlined by the fact that tax confidentiality in Germany is regarded a fundamental principle of the rule of law, and as one of the cornerstones of the AO.[142] Moreover, after the abuse of tax confidentiality under the regime of the national socialist, it was important for the legislator to ensure that this event would not occur again. However, next to the rationale of the protection of the individual taxpayer, another rationale is clarified in the historical development. After the abuse of tax confidentiality during the regime of national socialists, not only the benefit of the taxpayer due to tax confidentiality was of importance but also the interest of the tax administration. This was because, in case of a limited cooperation duty, the problem would have arisen that the taxpayer disregarded to disclose all relevant information and various tax sources could not have been used properly.[143] As a result, the legislator opted for tax confidentiality. Therefore, another rationale of the approach taken by the Germany legal system is public interest, specifically tax compliance, since tax confidentiality supports the collection of taxes. A taxpayer, knowing, that his information is to be disclosed, will most likely not present his full information to the tax authorities. This can be

---

[140] § 90; § 93; § 97 AO.

[141] Würtz 1999 (p.1), p. 4.

[142] Würtz 1999 (p.1), p. 3.

[143] Koch & Wolter 1958 (p.1), p. 6.

underlined by § 40 AO. According to § 40 of the AO, it is immaterial for taxation if an action that is taxable, violates a statutory regulation or prohibition or is, against public policy.[144] Without tax confidentiality, the taxpayer would be penalized for his offences or illegal acts he had enclosed voluntarily. Inevitably, this would lead to a general non-compliance, since taxpayers would not be willing to disclose information that would make them liable. Thus, tax confidentiality in Germany, therefore, has, besides the protection rationale, the rationale of tax compliance and an overall equal taxation.[145]

Derived from the historical development of tax confidentiality in the U.S., it can be observed that the debate about whether to disclose information or not, evoked several times. The focus in this debate has been on the aim of tax compliance, rather than on the protection of the taxpayer. During the enactments by the Congress, the attention was drawn on the impact of disclosure on the continuation of tax compliance in the voluntary assessment system of the United States.[146] Therefore, it can be concluded that the provisions, stipulating a high level of confidentiality, are based on the rationale of compliance. This is due to the fact, that a high level of confidentiality leads to better voluntary compliance, since the taxpayer knows that information revealed to the IRS is kept confidential. A tax return consists of information of sensitive and personal nature and taxpayer might feel exposed to embarrassment when these are disclosed and others can observe it.[147] However, if the taxpayer knows that the information ends with the government', it is acceptable.[148] In addition to that, in the U.S., the high degree of confidentiality is also based on the taxpayer's right to privacy, which can be observed by looking at the provision of tax confidentiality and furthermore at the Congress during the enactment of the Tax Reform Act 1976.[149]

Another aspect, according to Joshua Blank (2012), is the rationale of the approach of tax confidentiality being a form of strategic publicity function.[150]

---

[144] § 40 AO.

[145] Würtz 1999 (p.1), p. 3.

[146] Hambre 2015, p. 201.

[147] Blank 2013, p. 1.

[148] Hambre 2015, p. 268.

[149] Department of the Treasury 2012, p. 1-9.

[150] Blank 2012, p. 265.

Blank (2012) calls it the 'curtain of privacy' and argues that because of the information being confidential, the tax evasion investigation system of the IRS appears to be strict.[151] This is due to the method of the IRS, displaying its strengths namely the tax evasion cases it investigated without presenting its weaknesses. This method has the effect of deterrence, which is increased by every example of tax evasion that is published.[152] Although, it seems that the IRS follows a strict and accurate approach, this could change the moment every tax related information and case would be disclosed. Eventually, the assessment system of the IRS would appear to be not as accurate and effective, as it seems. This rationale, however, cannot be proven by the historical development or by any case law or other primary sources. Thus, it is not considered to be a primary rationale.

It can be concluded, that the approaches taken by Germany and the United States are similar, in that both have the rationale of taxpayer's privacy protection. However, in the United States it is more relevant to achieve tax compliance and might be a form of publicity strategy.

Conclusion

At first sight, it seems that the legal systems of Germany, as well as, the system of the U.S. apply a similar level of confidentiality. However, after interpreting the similarities and differences with respect to the development of tax confidentiality, its current legal framework and the rationale behind it, it becomes clear that the level of confidentiality in Germany is higher than in the U.S. Its historical development in Germany was rather static, whereas in the U.S., the pendulum swung from tax information disclosure to the prohibition of disclosure. Moreover, the legal provision of Germany only entails four exceptions to the general rule of confidentiality, whereas in the U.S. thirteen are present. Furthermore, the provision in the U.S. is not clear regarding tax information that has been public in court records. Subsequently, the decision, whether the disclosure of tax information in court records constitutes a violation of tax confidentiality, lies in the discretion of the Courts. Moreover, when it comes to the cooperation with the

---

[151] Blank 2012, p. 265.

[152] Blank 2012, p. 319.

media, in the U.S., the IRS can disclose taxpayer's information to the media, in case the taxpayer, alleged of tax infringements, cannot be located. This is, under no circumstances allowed in Germany, where such exception to tax confidentiality does not exist. However, the provision of the United States is clearer in relation to the definition of information, whereas in Germany a definition of 'circumstances of a third person' does not exist in the Fiscal Code.

Using the scale Hambre created in her article[153] on total tax confidentiality and complete tax transparency, the legal systems of Germany and the U.S. would lie close to total tax confidentiality, but not on the same level:

Germany   United States

Total tax confidentiality   Complete tax transparency

Hambre 2015, p. 166. Adapted by Nadja Büngers, 2017

With respect to the rationale, both countries emphasise the importance of confidentiality and consider it as a right since most tax information might be highly personal. However, Germany places higher emphasis on the protection of the taxpayer, whereas in the United States, tax compliance is the bigger objective of tax confidentiality. Even though, the argumentation of Blank (2012) of that the IRS uses tax confidentiality as a strategy tool in order to appear to have a strong system regarding tax evasion, it is regarded as a primary rationale in this thesis. This is due to the fact, that the argumentation, cannot be supported by either case law or other primary sources.

To answer the research question: 'How is tax related information of an individual taxpayer protected by tax confidentiality and what is the rationale behind it?',

tax related information is, in both, Germany and the United States, protected by one provision, implying the right to tax confidentiality, that prescribes the persons, who must keep the information confidential. This means, it is ensured that the information of the taxpayer does not reach the public domain. Furthermore, the provisions state exceptions when it is allowed and respectively necessary to disclose the information to another authority or to the public. In both jurisdictions,

---

[153] Hambre 2015, p. 166.

the violation confidentiality is penalized under the Criminal Code of the legal system.

The rationales found in this thesis are the protection of the taxpayer, as primarily followed by the German approach and the aim of tax compliance, mainly followed by the U.S. approach. All in all, the German system and the U.S. legal system hold a high level of confidentiality, however, Germany applies an even higher level than the U.S.

Bibliography

<u>Primary Sources</u>

Abgabenordnung

English version: The Fiscal Code of Germany retrieved from: <https://www.bundesfinanzministerium.de/Content/EN/Standardartikel/Ministry/ Laws/2015-01-01-fiscal-code.pdf?__blob=publicationFile&v=3> Last accessed on 12 July 2017

Act of 1934

Revenue Act of 1934, Chapter 277, Statute 680, 698

<http://www.constitution.org/uslaw/sal/048_itax.pdf> Last accessed on 12 July 2017

Freedom of Information Act 1966

Title 5 of United States Code Freedom of Information Act. 1966

Internal Revenue Code

Title 26 of United States Code Internal Revenue Code.

Gesetz über Steuerstatistiken [Law on Tax Statistics]

Strafgesetzbuch [German Criminal Code]

English version: Sascha Hardt and Nicole Kornet (eds.); *The Maastricht Collection. Selected National, European and International Provisions from Public and Private Law*, Volume 2, 5th Edition, Groningen: Europa Publishing, 2016.

<u>Case Law</u>

US

Church Scientology v IRS 792 F2d. 153 (U.S. Supreme Court 1987)

FBI v Albramson 456 US 615 (U.S. Supreme Court 1983)

Johnson v Sawyer 166 F3d. 1088 (5th Circuit Court of Appeals 1991)

Landmark Legal Foundation v IRS 267 F3d. 1132 (2001 DC Circuit)

Mallas v US 993 F2d 1111 (4ᵗʰ Circuit Court of Appeals 1994)

Renegotiation Board v Bannercraft Clothing 415 US 1 (U.S. Supreme Court 1974)

Rice v US 166 F3d 1088 (10ᵗʰ Circuit Court of Appeals 1999)

Rodgers v Hyatt 697 F2d. 899 (10ᵗʰ Circuit Court of Appeals 1863)

Rowley v U.S. 76 F3d. 796 (6ᵗʰ Circuit Court of Appeals 1996)

United States v Dickey [1925], 268, p. 386. (U.S. Supreme Court)

Germany

BFH, 25.04.1967, VII 151/60 (Bundesfinanzhof)

BFH, 08.02.1994, VII R 88/92 (Bundesfinanzhof)

BVerfG, 17.07.1984, 2 BvE 15/83 (Bundesverfassungsgericht)

Secondary sources

Ax et al. 2007

Rolf Ax et al.; *Abgabenordnung und Finanzgerichtsordnung.* Stuttgart: Schäfer-Poeschel Verlag, 2007

Blank 2012

Joshua Blank; 'In Defense of Individual Tax Privacy' *New York University Law and Economics Working Papers* (2012), p. 267-268

Blank 2013

Joshua Blank; 'United States National Report on Tax Privacy' *New York University School of Law Paper 33*, (2013), p. 1 - 28

Blank et al. 2013

Joshua Blank et al.; 'USA', in: Elenor Kristoffersson et al., (Eds.); *Tax Secrecy and Tax Transparency: The Relevance of Confidentiality in Tax Law.* Frankfurt: Peter Lang, 2013

Berggren 1999

Mark Berggren; 'I.R.C. §6103: Let's get to the 'Source' of the Problem'; Chicago-Kent Law Review Vol. 74, p. 825 – 853 Retrieved from: <http://scholarship.kentlaw.iit.edu/cgi/viewcontent.cgi?article=3284&context=ck lawreview> Last accessed on 12 July 2017

Department of Treasury 2012

Department of Treasury 'Disclosure and Privacy Law Reference Guide', *Internal Revenue Service Publication 4639 Catalogue 50891P* Retrieved from: <https://www.irs.gov/pub/irs-pdf/p4639.pdf> Last accessed on 12 July 2017

Hambre 2015

Anna Maria Hambre; 'Tax Confidentiality in Sweden and the United States – A Comparative *Study' International Journal of Legal Information Vol. 43.2-3*, p. 165 - 233

Internal Revenue Service 2015 [Manual]

Internal Revenue Service 2015; 'Internal Revenue Manual Part 11, Chapter 3, Section 11 (3) on Information which has become Public Record'; Retrieved from: <https://www.irs.gov/irm/part11/irm_11-003-011.html> last accessed on 12 July 2017

Internal Revenue Service 2017 [Manual]

Internal Revenue Service 2017; 'Internal Revenue Manual Part 11, Chapter 3 Section 13 on Freedom of Information Act'; Retrieved from: <https://www.irs.gov/irm/part11/irm_11-003-013.html#d0e2397> last accessed on 12 July 2017

Koch & Wolter 1958

Carl Koch & Björn Wolter; *Das Steuergeheimnis*. Köln: Verlag Dr. Otto Schmidt KG, 1958

Kristoffersson *et al.* 2013

Elenor Kristoffersson et al., (Eds.); *Tax Secrecy and Tax Transparency: The Relevance of Confidentiality in Tax Law*. Frankfurt: Peter Lang, 2013

Lenter & Shackelford & Slemrod 2003

David Lenter; 'Public Disclosure of Corporate Tax Return Information: Accounting, Economics, and Legal Perspectives', *National Tax Law Vol. 56, No.4* (2003), p. 803 - 830 Retrieved from: <https://www.ntanet.org/NTJ/56/4/ntj-v56n04p803-30-public-disclosure-corporate-tax.pdf> Last accessed on 12 July 2017

Mehany & Michel & Rizek 2015 [Report]

Dianne C. Mehany & Scott D. Michel & Christopher S. Rizek; 'United States – Branch Report', IFA, p. 873 – 894

Metzger & Weingarten 1989

Ulrike Metzger & Joe Weingarten; *Einkommensteuer und Einkommensteuerverwaltung in Deutschland: Ein historischer und verwaltungswissenschaftlicher Überblick*. Wiesbaden: Springer Fachmedien Wiesbaden GmbH, 1989

Office of Tax Policy, Department of the Treasury 2000

Office of Tax Policy Department of the Treasury, Report to the Congress on Scope and Use of Taxpayer Confidentiality and Disclosure Provisions, Volume I: Study of General Provisions, Washington, 2000 Retrieved from: <https://www.treasury.gov/resource-center/tax-policy/Documents/Report-Taxpayer-Confidentiality-2010.pdf > Last accessed on 12 July 2017

Office of the Treasury Inspector General for Tax Administration 2015

Office of the Treasury Inspector General for Tax Administration, 'Operations Manual, Chapter 700 on I.R.C. §6103' (2015) Retrieved from: <https://www.treasury.gov/tigta/important_foia_ad_oper.shtml#7>, Last accessed on 12 July 2017

Petersen 2005

Jens Petersen; *Das Bankgeheimnis zwischen Individualschutz und Insitutionschutz*. Tübigen: Mohr Siebeck, 2005

Pfaff 1984

Paul Pfaff; *Kommentar zum Steuergeheimnis*. Berlin: Duncker und Humblot, 1974

Pollack 2013

Sheldon D. Pollack; 'The first National Income Tax, 1861 – 1872' *Tax Lawyer Vol. 66 No. 2*, p. 295 – 330

Ruegenberg 2001

Guido Ruegenberg; *Das nationale und internationale Steuergeheimnis im Schnittpunkt von Besteuerungs- und Strafverfahren*. Köln: Verlag Dr. Otto Schmidt KG, 2001

Russell 2015

Irma Russell; 'The Evolving Balance of Transparency and Privacy in open Government', *Open Journals Revue IMODEV* Vol. 2 (2015), <http://ojs.imodev.org/index.php/RIGO/article/view/12/75>, Last accessed on 12 July 2017

Schwartz 2008

Paul Schwartz; 'The Future of Tax Privacy', *National Tax Journal Vol. LXI, No. 4* (2008), p. 833 - 900

Senate 1965

Senate Report No. 813, 89th Congress, 1st Session (1965), Retrieved from: <http://nsarchive.gwu.edu/nsa/foialeghistory/S.%20Rep.%20No.%2089-813%20(1966%20Source%20Book).pdf> Last accessed on 12 July 2017

Thuronyi 2016

Victor Thuronyi; *Comparative Tax Law*. Second Edition, The Hague: Wolters Kluwer Law, 2016

Twight 1995

Charlotte Twight; 'Evolution of the Federal Income Tax Withholding: The Machinery of Institutional Change', *Cato Journal Vol. 14* (1995) p. 359 - 395

United Nations Conference on Trade and Development 2016

United Nations Conference on Trade and Development, 'Data protection regulations and international data flows: Implications for trade and development', *United Nations*, 2016. Retrieved from: <http://unctad.org/en/PublicationsLibrary/dtlstict2016d1_en.pdf> Last accessed on 12 July 2017

Valta *et al.* 2013

Matthias Valta et al.; 'Germany', in: Elenor Kristoffersson et al., (Eds.); *Tax Secrecy and Tax Transparency: The Relevance of Confidentiality in Tax Law*. Frankfurt: Peter Lang, 2013

Würtz 1999

M. Würtz, *Das Steuergeheimnis: §30- Abgabenordnung, Studienarbeit*. München: Grin Verlag, 1999

Tertiary Sources

Ernst & Young 2013

Ernst & Young, 'Ernst & Young LLP: Tax Transparency: Seizing the Initiative' (2013),   Retrieved   from: <http://www.ey.com/Publication/vwLUAssets/Tax_Transparency_-_Seizing_the_initiative/$FILE/EY_Tax_Transparency.pdf> Last accessed on 12 July 2017

Federal Ministry of Justice Germany 2016

Federal Ministry of Justice, 'An ABC of Taxes', *Federal Ministry of Justice* (2016), Retrieved from: <http://www.howtogermany.com/files/2012-10-30-abc-on-taxes.pdf > Last accessed on 12 July 2017

Schoon 2014

André Schoon, 'Das Steuergeheimnis' (2014), p. 1- 11 Retrieved from: <https://www.rosepartner.de/fileadmin/Redaktion/PDFs/Steuergeheimnis.docx.pdf> Last accessed on 12 July 2017

YOUR KNOWLEDGE HAS VALUE

Lightning Source UK Ltd.
Milton Keynes UK
UKHW01f0611310518
323512UK00001B/212/P

9 783668 567740